THE AMAZING HIS...
HOMES

T0011111

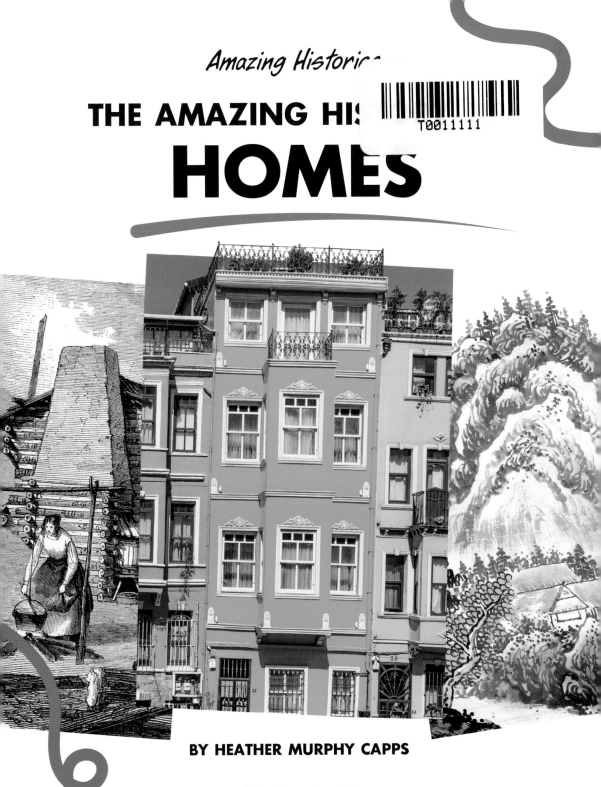

BY HEATHER MURPHY CAPPS

CAPSTONE PRESS
a capstone imprint

Published by Capstone Press, an imprint of Capstone.
1710 Roe Crest Drive, North Mankato, Minnesota 56003
capstonepub.com

Library of Congress Cataloging-in-Publication Data is available on the Library of Congress website.
ISBN: 9781669011965 (hardcover)
ISBN: 9781669011910 (paperback)
ISBN: 9781669011927 (ebook PDF)

Summary: The homes we live in today look a lot different than they did in the past. From caves to castles to the invention of indoor bathrooms, the history of homes is surprising, unusual, and amazing. Learn more about how people used these innovations to survive and thrive in everyday life.

Editorial Credits
Editor: Alison Deering; Designer: Jaime Willems; Media Researcher: Donna Metcalf; Production Specialist: Tori Abraham

Image Credits
Alamy: De Luan, 18; Getty Images: Alexander Spatari, back cover top left (colorful houses), Alexander Spatari, cover middle, 1, AOtzen, 27, Elizabeth Beard, 14-15, Jean-Philippe Tournut, 17, Sonja Grunbauer, 23, abdelfatah, 13, baoyan, cover right, 1, Hannamariah, 5, keunhyungkim, 29, LiteHeavy, 6, MarcoAAAraujo, 9, Marzolino, cover left, 1, MaxMaximovPhotography, 11, Mega Pixel, cover top left (blueprint background), Pakenee Kittipinyowat, 24, patpitchaya, 25, Roman Motizov, cover top left (blueprint overlay), SCStock, 16, VITALII BORKOVSKYI, cover top left (building level), Volodymyr Nikitenko, 10, ZhannaZviagina, back cover top left (Machu Picchu), 21

All internet sites appearing in back matter were available and accurate when this book was sent to press.

Printed and bound in the USA. PO 5195

TABLE OF
CONTENTS

HISTORY OF HOMES 4

WELCOME TO THE STONE AGE 6

TOILETS AND TOOLS 8

OUTDOOR LIVING 12

MIDDLE AGES 16

HOMES AROUND THE WORLD 20

SMALL SPACES 26

GLOSSARY 30

READ MORE 31

INTERNET SITES 31

INDEX 32

ABOUT THE AUTHOR 32

Words in **BOLD** are in the glossary.

HISTORY OF
HOMES

Whether you live in a house or a castle, an apartment or condo, all homes have something in common. They share the same amazing and sometimes gross history.

WELCOME TO
THE STONE AGE

The first homes were simple. Early humans needed to stay safe from wild animals and bad weather. They slept in caves, rock shelters, or even tall trees.

Ancient shelters were built using animal skins and bones.

Ancient people also built round huts or teepees. They used stones and **mammoth** bones to make walls. Some used animal **hides** to help block the wind.

DID YOU KNOW?

Historians believe early humans went to the bathroom outside, usually in a hole. Ick!

TOILETS AND TOOLS

Early homes didn't have much furniture. But there was one important seat—the toilet!

In ancient Greece, some homes had flushing toilets—sort of. There was no running water. Instead, people poured buckets of water into the toilet. It emptied into the main city drain.

Some ancient bathroom seats were made of stone.

Home Building Tools

By 3000 BCE, humans began using metal tools. They used sharp axes to cut down trees. Trees were used to build homes.

Homes can be found high above the water near the Alps in Germany and other countries.

People who lived near rivers and lakes needed to stay dry. They built houses on tree trunks that stood above the water. Floors were made of smaller logs. The logs were covered with smooth mud.

OUTDOOR
LIVING

People in the Middle East and Egypt found ways to stay cool. They lived in houses with flat roofs. The roofs provided a cooler place to cook and sleep.

These houses were usually made of mud bricks. In Egypt, this clay mud came from the Nile River. Clay helped keep houses cool.

The remains of an ancient village in Egypt

Apartment Life

Many people in ancient Rome lived in apartments. Buildings were usually five to seven floors high. They had six or seven apartments. They housed about 40 people.

Each building usually had a courtyard in the center. People went there to stay cool. They also cooked there.

The ruins of an ancient apartment building in Rome

MIDDLE
AGES

A bridge leads to Huyad Castle in Romania.

What's the difference between a palace and a castle? Royals built palaces to live in luxury. They were filled with fine art and furniture.

In the Middle Ages, rulers built stone castles to protect their lands. They were more like sturdy forts. Soldiers, **moats**, and tall walls kept out enemies. Some, like Windsor Castle in England, still stand today.

DID YOU KNOW?
In 518 BCE, Persian king Darius the Great built Persepolis. It was one of the first palaces in the world.

Smoke and Stink

Most people in the Middle Ages lived in homes made of wood. Families cooked over a fire inside the main common area. Homes had large holes in the roofs to let out smoke. Most homes were stinky and smoky.

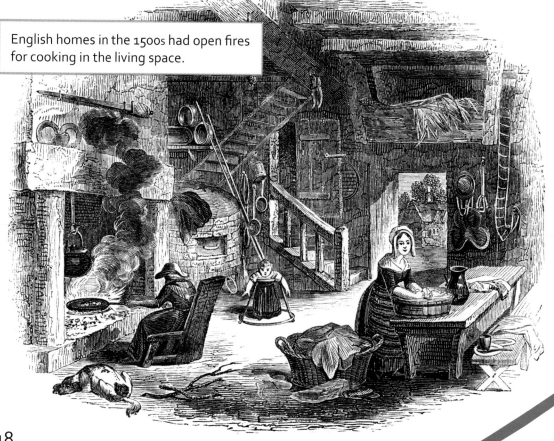

English homes in the 1500s had open fires for cooking in the living space.

Windows were just holes in the walls. Glass was too expensive for most people. While these windows let in fresh air, they also let in the cold. Brrr!

DID YOU KNOW?

By the 1500s, glass was less expensive. But if you had glass windows, you took them with you when you moved to a new house!

HOMES AROUND
THE WORLD

By the late 1600s, most homes were made of stone or brick. **Masons** used sharp tools to cut blocks out of stone. It was hard work. But these homes were warmer, drier, and safer.

In Peru, masons fit stones close together to build strong **foundations**. These foundations never cracked, even during earthquakes.

DID YOU KNOW?

Great Zimbabwe was a city in southern Africa. Masons there built a royal home using more than 1 million blocks of stone!

Tight stonework can be seen in Machu Picchu, Peru.

Painted Houses

In South Africa, the Ndebele have a unique **tradition**. Women use chicken feathers to paint their homes. They create strong patterns with thick black lines and bold colors. These designs have different meanings. Some show the family is important.

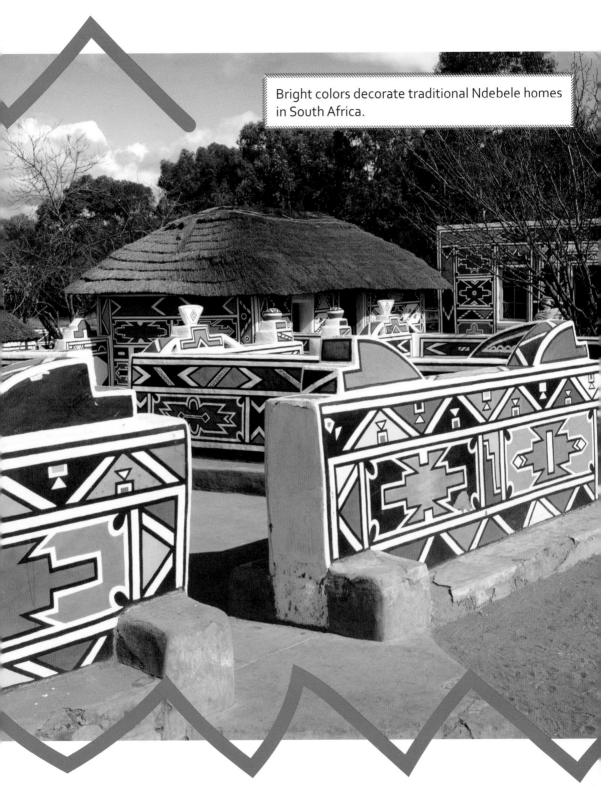

Bright colors decorate traditional Ndebele homes in South Africa.

Finding Harmony

In China, many homes are built facing south. That's because of **feng shui**. It's the art of arranging buildings and objects. The goal is to create harmony and balance. This tradition has been around for more than 4,000 years.

Doors and lanterns outside a traditional Chinese home

Feng shui fish chimes represent richness.

SMALL
SPACES

In the 1800s, many **pioneers** in the United States and Canada moved west. They used prairie grass **sod** to build homes.

People cut blocks of grass from the ground. They stacked these sod "bricks" into walls and roofs. These homes were usually small. They had just one or two rooms.

A house made of sod stands in Jackson, Minnesota.

DID YOU KNOW?

A sod house was sometimes called a "soddy."

City Life

Over time, cities around the world grew. People needed houses, but there wasn't as much space to go around. The answer? Apartment buildings. These have been around since ancient Roman times!

GLOSSARY

feng shui (FUHNG SHWEY)—a Chinese practice in which a home is arranged or designed to create harmony and balance

foundation (foun-DAY-shuhn)—a solid structure on which a building is built

hide (HYDE)—the skin of an animal

mammoth (MAM-uhth)—a very large, hairy extinct elephant with long tusks that curved upward

mason (MEY-suhn)—a person who builds or works with stone or brick

moat (MOHT)—a deep, wide ditch dug all around a castle or fort and filled with water to prevent attacks

pioneer (pye-uh-NEER)—a person who is among the first to settle a new land

sod (SOD)—the top layer of soil and the grass attached to it

tradition (truh-DISH-uhn)—a custom, idea, or belief passed down through time

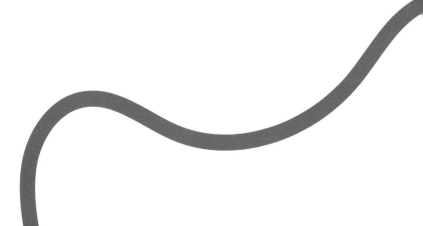

READ MORE

Higgins, Nadia. *Homes Then and Now*. Minneapolis: Jump!, Inc., 2019.

Laroche, Giles. *If You Lived Here: Houses of the World*. New York: Houghton Mifflin Books for Children, 2011.

Lawrence, Carol. *Homes from Then to Now*. Chicago: Albert Whitman and Company, 2021.

INTERNET SITES

Ancient Mesopotamia for Kids
mesopotamia.mrdonn.org/homes.html

DK Find Out!: Houses in the Indus Cities
dkfindout.com/us/history/indus-valley-civilization/houses-in-indus-cities

Easy Science for Kids: Pile Dwellings of the Alps
easyscienceforkids.com/all-about-pile-dwellings-of-the-alps

INDEX

apartments, 4, 14, 15, 28

bricks, 12

Canada, 26
castles, 4, 16
caves, 6
China, 24
courtyards, 15

early humans, 6, 7
Egypt, 12, 13
England, 17

feng shui, 24, 25
floors, 11
foundations, 20

glass, 19
Greece, 8

huts, 7

mammoths, 7
masons, 20
Middle East, 12
moats, 17
mud, 11, 12

palaces, 17
Peru, 20
pioneers, 26

Rome, 14–15, 28
roofs, 12, 18, 26

sod, 26, 27
South Africa, 20, 22, 23

teepees, 7
toilets, 8
tools, 10
trees, 6, 10, 11

United States, 26

walls, 7, 17, 19, 26
windows, 19

ABOUT THE AUTHOR

photo credit: Jody McKitrick

Heather Murphy Capps grew up in a small Minnesota town where the motto is, "Cows, Colleges, and Contentment." She spent 20 years as a television news journalist before deciding to focus on her favorite kind of writing: books for kids involving history, social justice, science, magic, and a touch of mystery. She's a mixed-race author committed to diversity in publishing, an administrator/contributor to the blog From the Mixed-Up Files . . . of Middle-Grade Authors, and the author of the middle grade novel *Indigo and Ida* (Lerner/Carolrhoda Lab). Heather now lives in northern Virginia with her husband, two kids, and two cats.